# I Know It
# When
# I See It

# I Know It When I See It

A Modern Fable About Quality

John Guaspari

## amacom
American Management Association

This book is available at a special discount when ordered in bulk quantities. For information, contact Special Sales Department, AMACOM, a division of American Management Association, 135 West 50th Street, New York, NY 10020.

Library of Congress Cataloging in Publication Data

Guaspari, John.
  I know it when I see it.

    1. Industrial management— Miscellanea. 2. Quality control— Miscellanea. 3. Quality of products—Miscellanea. I. Title.
    HD38.G766   1985      658.5'62
    84-45814
    ISBN 0-8144-5787-8

Design by Sheryl Farber

Printing number

10  9  8  7  6  5  4  3  2  1

*For Gail*

# Acknowledgments

There are literally scores of colleagues at GenRad, Inc., whose ideas and observations over the past six years have contributed greatly to whatever insights this book has to offer. My thanks to all of them.

I'd especially like to thank Bob Anderson, John Ferrie, and John Hurley, without whose assistance and encouragement this book would not have been published.

John Guaspari

# Prologue

*Once upon a time the English language was very dull     Flat     Lifeless*

*It was perfectly functional   perfectly utilitarian*

*But it didnt sing*

*It didnt shine*

*A typical sentence would sound like this one     And then the next one would sound like this one     And the next one like this*

*And it would go on and on in a similar way*

*The same was true for both written and spoken English*

*There was no poetry*

*There were no songs*

*There were no records kept of all this*
  *Thats because people didnt want to bother handing down such flat lifeless prose to their descendants*
  *For which we should all be very grate ful*




  Rufus Punctum lived a long time ago. No one is quite sure about exactly when that was. It you've gotten this far, then you know why.
  Anyway, it was a long time ago, and legend says that Rufus enjoyed life a lot.
  He felt happiness.
  He felt sadness.
  He felt pain.
  He felt joy.
  He felt all those things and more.
  Most of all, he felt deeply. But when he tried to explain those feelings to other people, all the feelings went behind the door and hid.
  He would say things like:

  *That was a very moving experi ence      I feel great gladness and joy*

Or:

  *The pain in the corn on my foot is excruciating*

Or:

> *I very much hate having to speak in
> such a wooden manner*

And the people listening to Rufus would
say:

> *I am very pleased that you are feel
> ing such gladness and joy*

Or:

> *Perhaps some epsom salts would
> be of help*

Or:

> *I do not understand why you think
> speaking in the manner to which we
> have become accustomed should
> be characterized as being wooden*

And Rufus would feel a gnawing in his
stomach.

That, at least, would take his mind off
his corns.


One night Rufus got on his knees and
said the same simple prayer he always said:

> *Please   God   let   somebody   figure*

*out a way to make our language
less bland and boring*

Then he pulled back the covers and climbed into bed.

But he couldn't sleep. So he got out of bed and went to his writing table in a mood of despair. Putting pen to paper, he wrote:

*Why must the language be so inade quate for communicating true feeling and emotion?*

He stopped and read what he had written. Then he wrote:

*What was that odd curving mark I made at the end of that last sen tence?*

Again he stopped and read what he had written.

This time he smiled.

Thus was punctuation discovered.

unctuation Inc. was a fabulously successful enterprise.

That's not surprising. Because if people wanted to do anything more daring than capitalizing the beginning of a sentence, they needed Punctuation.

The company had a broad line of products:

Commas, apostrophes, and periods.
Question marks, exclamation points, and dashes.
Parentheses and brackets.
Semicolons and colons.
Even luxury items like ellipses.

All were marks of Punctuation. And there was a broad range of markets. The company sold to:

Consumers, who needed a lot of exclamation points to put after words like "Golly!" and "Wow!"

Lawyers, who bought commas by the carload to put after all their "whereas" clauses.

Doctors, for whom a special line of punctuation marks was created, legible only to pharmacists.

Comic-strip artists, who couldn't use profanity in family newspapers.

Businesspeople, who preferred semi-colons to colons by a wide margin after buying committees made the compromise, consensus choice.

The list of customers went on and on.

And there were plenty of imitators too, plenty of competitors who offered the same "kinds" of products. But they all could trace their origins directly to Punctuation's door.

And none of them could ever hold a candle to the sheer power, genius, and innovation that had been shown by Rufus Punctum and his descendants in commerce.

Yes, Punctuation Inc. was a powerful commercial enterprise. But its impact and contributions to society went much deeper than the bottom line.

Think of the thousands of lives that have been saved since it became possible for the simple statement "Fire" to become the urgent cry of "Fire!!!"

Punctuation Inc. made that possible.

Think of the important role that radio operators using Morse code played during both world wars. Where do you think they got all those dots and dashes?

Think of the effect on our literary heritage. Why, for example, without Punctuation Inc., we still wouldn't know whether the Raven quoth "Nevermore!" or just kept his beak shut and quoth nevermore!

Yes, we have the folks at Punctuation Inc. to thank for all that and more.

They were dominant.

They were admirable.

They were invincible.

Or so they thought.

Of course, the dominance of Punctuation Inc. did not go unchallenged.

Every day, it seemed, a new challenger would appear on the scene.

First there had been Excite Inc., which specialized in exclamation points. (They did very well for a while. But then OSHA closed them down because of the noise level in their factory.)

Then came Interrogation Inc.—question mark specialists. (Indecisiveness eventually finished them off.)

There had even been a black market for people who wanted to lie, dissemble, and renege on deals. A shady company called Disappear Inc. catered to them. (These punctuation marks seemed perfectly fine when written or spoken. But within minutes, they would vanish without a trace. After the grand jury hearing, so did Disappear Inc.)

The list of would-be competitors goes

on. Each would catch the public fancy for a short time with a new gimmick or a cut-rate product. But before long, each would disappear.

No, Punctuation Inc. was the place to go for punctuation. They had the reputation. The innovation. The broad product line. The lead (by a wide margin) in market share.

They were the one constant.

Or so they thought.

But then, one day, The Boss looked over the quarterly sales reports, and an unfamiliar name caught his eye.

Oh, he saw Punctuation Inc. on top all right. But in second place he saw a new rival called Process Inc.

He called his right-hand man into his office.

"What do you know about Process Inc.?" asked The Boss.

"I think they're number two," said the right-hand man. "In fact, I think they've been number two for four straight quarters now."

The right-hand man sensed that this was not welcome news to The Boss. And he did not like giving The Boss bad news.

"I wouldn't worry about it, though," he continued, trying to put The Boss (and himself) at ease. "After all, somebody has to be number two. It might as well be Process Inc.

In time they'll fade out of sight like all the rest. You'll see."

"I hope you're right," said The Boss.

But the right-hand man wasn't.


Process Inc. stayed in second place for six straight quarters. That was bad enough.

But what really bothered The Boss was that Process Inc. had gained market share for ten straight quarters—at Punctuation Inc.'s expense.

And that had never happened before.

The Boss called in his left-hand man and asked him what he thought.

"Don't worry, Boss," said the left-hand man. "Process Inc. is no threat to us. All they do is make cheap knockoffs of our products. They've never had an original idea."

"But they're gaining market share!" said The Boss. "They're taking customers away from us!"

"They'll come back to us," said the left-hand man. "And anyway, if people can't see that we're the ones with the brains and the know-how, then I say who needs 'em? We'll still be number one. Let them go to Process Inc. Remember, somebody's got to be number two, right?"

"Right," said The Boss.

Somebody's got to be number two, he thought.

And that's what worried him.

So The Boss decided to do some market research.

He went to a nearby stationery store and waited in the punctuation department. (So dominant was Punctuation Inc. that that's what such departments were always called.)

His plan was to wait there for people to buy punctuation from Process Inc. instead of from Punctuation Inc. and then ask them why.

He didn't have to wait long.

First came a woman with two young children in tow. She walked directly by the Punctuation Inc. display and proceeded to the products of Process Inc.

There she selected two Family Packs from Process Inc.: a dozen each of commas, periods, question marks, and exclamation points. No frills. No extras.

The Boss approached her. "Excuse me," he said, "but I noticed that you chose the Family Pack from Process Inc. May I ask why?"

"Because I have young children," she replied, "and I need to be able to communicate in a very simple, effective way. I've got to be able to count on their understanding. Excuse me a moment."

And with that she turned toward her young daughter, who had begun to wander off.

"Jennifer," she said, calmly and clearly. No strain, no shouting. "Come back."

And Jennifer did.

"Anyway," the woman continued, turning her attention back to The Boss, "these seem to work better."

"But," asked The Boss, "do you realize that Punctuation Inc. offers a similar product?"

"Yes, but . . ." the woman began. Before she could complete her answer, her young son began to pull another Family Pack off the shelf.

"Jeremy," the woman said, calmly and clearly. No shouting, no strain. "Put that back."

And Jeremy did.

"As I was saying," the woman continued, "I guess you'd have to say it's because of Quality."

That was just about the *last* answer The Boss expected to hear.

"Have you ever tried Punctuation Inc.'s products?" he asked.

"Yes, I have," answered the woman.

"And?" prompted The Boss.

"And they just didn't seem to work as well," answered the woman.

"How do you mean?" probed The Boss.

"I don't know—the Quality just wasn't as good," shrugged the woman.

"And just how would you define Quality?" pried The Boss (in, perhaps, a slightly

, , ,    • • •    ? ? ?    ! ! !
, , ,    • • •    ? ? ?    ! ! !
, , ,    • • •    ? ? ?    ! ! !
, , ,    • • •    ? ? ?    ! ! !


, , ,    • • •    ? ? ?    ! ! !
, , ,    • • •    ? ? ?    ! ! !
, , ,    • • •    ? ? ?    ! ! !
, , ,    • • •    ? ? ?    ! ! !

sharper tone than the interests of pure, dispassionate market research might have called for).

The woman shrugged again. "I guess I'd just have to say that I know it when I see it."

The Boss thanked her for her time. Then she went off, with Jennifer and Jeremy happily under control.

The Boss found all this *very* exasperating.

She was choosing one product over the other—passing up the original at that—all because of Quality.

But when he asked her what Quality meant to her, all she could say was, "I know it when I see it."

How was he supposed to run a business that catered to people like that?

To make matters worse, it went on like that all day. Different people from different walks of life, with different punctuation needs, were all buying from Process Inc.:

FM disk jockeys, who needed to be mellow.

Schoolteachers, who needed to be precise.

Traffic cops, who needed to be authoritative.

Engineers, who wrote (and sometimes spoke) in scientific notation.

Members of the clergy, who needed to be sympathetic.

Bartenders, who needed to be empa-
thetic.

Panhandlers, for whom simply pa-
thetic was enough.

Air traffic controllers, who needed to be
unfailingly accurate.

Day care instructors, who needed to
show patience and cheerfulness.

Marine Corps drill instructors, who
didn't.

On and on it went.

And when The Boss asked all of them
why they bought from Process Inc., he got
the same answer.

"Quality," they all said. Uncanny.

And when he asked them to define
what they meant by Quality, he got the
same answer too.

"I know it when I see it," they all said.
Uncannier.

The Boss felt mixed emotions.

He seemed to be onto something, and
that was good.

But "I know it when I see it" wasn't
much to run a business on.

Or so he thought.

The next day The Boss returned to his office. He felt much better than he had the day before.

Apparently the issue was Quality. That's what people wanted—even though they weren't really sure what it was.

Giving them Quality should be a snap. After all, doing higher-quality work just meant trying harder, doing better!

The Boss had always done high-quality work. That's how he had gotten to be The Boss!

And even now that he was The Boss, he was still helping out with Quality.

Why, just last week a crate of question marks was on the loading dock, ready to be shipped to a customer who had ordered commas.

If the shipment had gone out, busy people who wanted to accomplish long lists of tasks and who needed commas to separate the items on the lists would have gotten question marks instead. So rather than getting all their work done quickly, they'd have been stopping to question themselves all along the way.

It would have been a Quality disaster!

But during one of his weekly visits with the workers in the shipping department, The Boss had spotted the mix-up and avoided the problem.

And it had taken virtually no effort!

So if everyone *really* tried harder, did better—wouldn't Quality improve?

"That will be my top priority," vowed The Boss, "telling people to 'Try Harder! Do Better!' Then we'll have better Quality, and people won't have any reason to buy from Process Inc. anymore!"

Or so he thought.

o The Boss got on the PA system to address all of Punctuation Inc.'s employees.

"Attention, everyone. This is The Boss speaking."

And people stopped what they were doing and turned to face the speakers mounted on the walls throughout the building.

They were happy for the break and happy to hear from The Boss. They respected and admired him. If The Boss had something to say, they were ready to listen.

"You all know," said The Boss, "that Punctuation Inc. has been fabulously successful over the years."

"Hooray!" shouted the workers. The Boss could hear their cheers in his office, and he was pleased.

"Most of you also know," continued The Boss, "that we have been getting stiff competition from a company called Process Inc."

"Boo!" shouted the workers.

"All they do is copy what we do!"

"We have all the ideas!"

That too made The Boss smile.

He continued: "I have done some extensive market research to find out why this is happening, and I think I have the answer."

"Hooray for The Boss!" shouted the workers.

The Boss smiled again.

"The issue seems to be Quality," he said. "So starting today, Punctuation Inc. will produce higher-quality products than anyone else!"

"Three cheers for The Boss!"

"Hip-hip-hooray!"

"Hip-hip-hooray!!"

"Hip-hip-hooray!!!" shouted the workers.

The Boss was grinning now.

"And now I'm going to tell you how we're going to get better Quality!" enthused The Boss.

It was so quiet you could hear a comma drop. In fact, one did.

Plinck.

The workers were all breathless in anticipation.

They knew The Boss had found the secret. And he was about to share it with them. And soon Process Inc. would be only a memory.

Oh, hooray for The Boss, hooray!

"The secret is," said The Boss, preparing to hit them with his knockout punch as the workers leaned forward expectantly:

"Try Harder! Do Better!"

And then he waited for the reaction.

But there was none. At least none that he could hear.

In fact, it was still quiet enough to hear a comma drop, but for a different reason this time.

The workers were stunned.

"Try HARDER?!?" someone finally said.

"Doesn't he think we already try our hardest?"

"DO BETTER?!?" said someone else. "At what? At getting shipments out on time? Or at making sure a product works? Do better at *what?!?*"

"Try Harder!?! Do Better!?!" shouted all the workers.

The Boss could hear the shouts loud and clear.

And the silence that followed came through even louder and clearer.

Which was not the reaction he had expected.

The old feeling returned—the feeling he'd had when all that customers would tell him about Quality was "I know it when I see it."

How was he supposed to run a company whose employees were so unpredictable? Who would have thought they'd have reacted so negatively to the simple charge to try a little harder, do a little better?

These and a thousand other thoughts raced around in The Boss's head.

Clearly some rethinking was in order.

But there wasn't time now.

Because all the workers at Punctuation Inc. were still staring at the PA system's speakers, waiting to hear what else he had to say.

And if they weren't completely disgruntled, they were certainly a lot less gruntled than they had been.

So he had to say something, if only to put an end to this current little drama. He pushed the "speak" button on his microphone and said:

"Try Harder! Do Better! . . . Have a nice day!!"

The workers went back to work.

The Boss put the microphone down and sat back in his chair, consoling himself that even if his pep talk hadn't been a big hit, at least it hadn't done any harm.

Or so he thought.

he Boss's pep talk did have an effect.

Now, not only were sales down and market share down and profits down—

But morale was down too.

One long-time employee had even left Punctuation Inc. to go to work for—yes—Process Inc.!

On her last day with the company she had gone to The Boss and said, "I had wanted to help you solve the problems that Process Inc. was causing us. Then you came on the PA system and as much as told me that I was part of the problem!"

That, more than anything, had really bothered The Boss.

"Talk about taking a bad situation and making it worse," he said to himself. "How's *that* for leadership!"

He shook his head ruefully.

Then he called for his right-hand man and his left-hand man.

"The workers are upset," said The Boss to his right-hand man and his left-hand man after they had joined him in his office. "And they have a right to be.

"Good people want to do good work. Quality work. And these are good people. But people—even good people—make mistakes. Good intentions aren't enough.

"Try Harder! Do Better! isn't enough.

"How can we get better Quality if we have good people who are already doing their best?

"What's missing? What do we need to provide?"

From his tone, it was clear that The Boss had an answer in mind.

The right-hand man and the left-hand man each took a stab at what that answer was.

"More rewards?" suggested the right-hand man.

The Boss shook his head no.

"More threats?" offered the left-hand man.

The Boss shook his head again.

"No," he said, "rewards and threats won't work. Those are motivators. But the workers don't need motivation. They need leadership. And it's our job to provide it!"

The right-hand man and the left-hand man nodded their agreement.

The Boss continued: "Our customers— I should say our ex-customers—are telling us that Quality, whatever that is, is the key. So we've got to provide Quality, and we've got to provide it now!"

The right-hand man and the left-hand man thought The Boss was overreacting. But there was something about The Boss's tone that made them listen a bit more carefully than they might have otherwise.

"People are only human," said The Boss. "Mistakes are inevitable. The key to improving Quality is in catching those mis-

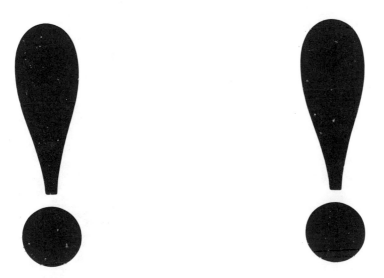

takes as soon as they occur. And how are we going to catch mistakes as soon as they occur?"

This time the right-hand man and the left-hand man were on the same wave-length as The Boss.

"More inspection!?!" they said in unison.

"That's right." The Boss nodded. "More inspection. Starting today, we're going to double the work force."

"Double the work force?" said the left-and right-hand men in unison.

"That's right. Double the work force," said The Boss. "We're going to hire another worker for every one that we have now. And do you know what the new workers are going to do?"

They didn't.

"They're going to inspect everything that the old workers do, as soon as they do it. That way mistakes will get caught as soon as they occur! Nothing will slip through!

"We're going to overpower our Quality problems with more inspection!!

"And just to show how much I value your contributions, as a vote of confidence, I won't be hiring any new people to watch the two of you!"

The left-hand man and the right-hand man were pleased. And relieved. Prematurely.

"You two," said The Boss triumphantly, "can inspect each other!"

**A**mazingly, a month later things were worse than ever.

Profits were down.

Market share was down (lost, of course, to Process Inc.).

Morale was down.

The Boss was down.

About the only thing that was up was the size of the work force.

"How," said The Boss to his left-hand man and his right-hand man, "could that be? We've got people whose sole job it is to catch mistakes. Yet there are more mistakes than ever. We were going to overpower our Quality problems. Yet our Quality problems are worse than ever. Where did we go wrong?"

But neither one answered. He tried again.

"Where," he asked, "did we go wrong?"

Again, silence.

"Where, gentlemen," The Boss asked

for the third time, with a sharper edge to his voice, "did we go wrong?"

And now the right-hand man looked at the left-hand man, and the left-hand man looked at the right-hand man.

"I thought you had the answer!" each said to the other, in unison.

"Today's your day to do the work and my day to do the checking!" said the right-hand man to the left-hand man.

"No, it's not. It's your day to do the work and my day to do the checking!" said the left-hand man to the right-hand man.

"Well, if it's your day to do the checking, then why don't you check and see which one of us is right?" said the right-hand man to the left-hand man.

"Because I figured that if I made a mistake, you'd catch it. After all, that's your job!" said the left-hand man to the right-hand man.

"Not today!" said the right-hand man to the left-hand man.

"Yes, today!" said the left-hand man to the right-hand man.

Who's on first? thought The Boss. He no longer had to ask where things had gone wrong. He could see it for himself.

Here were his two most trusted workers.

Neither knew what his job was anymore.

Neither one had responsibility anymore—each just assumed the other, acting as inspector, would catch his mistakes.

The Boss imagined the little scene that had just been played out before him repeated every day, with every worker. Twice as many workers as before.

No wonder Quality is down, he thought.

And morale is down.

And productivity is down.

And profitability is down.

And market share is down.

No wonder people weren't performing as well on their jobs. The Boss had made it impossible for people to know where their jobs left off and the next person's job began.

What was The Boss to do?

y now The Boss had arrived at several conclusions.

Above all, he had decided that Quality was nothing less than a matter of survival.

Of that he was certain. (And should a shadow of doubt tiptoe in, one look at the market share figures would shoo it away.)

Yet Try Harder! Do Better! wasn't the answer.

And More Inspection! wasn't the answer.

The Boss was more discouraged than ever.

He had tried to solve the Quality problems and had succeeded only in making things worse.

Morale was worse than ever. And now he had twice as many people whose morale was down!

No. His plan to overpower the Quality problem through massive inspection had been a failure in all respects but one: The only thing it had succeeded in doing was to dramatically increase the number of defects.

"Everybody figured," The Boss told himself, "that somebody else would catch the mistakes. And that just guaranteed that there would be mistakes to catch."

That insight led him to ruefully assert The Boss's corollary to Parkinson's law:

*In a closed system, the number of mistakes made expands to fill the inspection capacity available.*

He smiled at the irony as he showed his corollary to his right-hand man and his left-hand man.

"If my corollary is correct," he said, "then we've devised a system in which it's guaranteed that more mistakes than ever will be made. And there is nothing we can do about it—unless, of course, we change the system."

"Unless, of course, we change the system," shrugged the right-hand man, despondent.

"Unless, of course, we change the system," nodded the left-hand man in sympathetic assent.

The Boss stopped them cold with an excited shout.

"Unless, of course, we change The System!" he shouted, excitedly.

"Of course!" said the right-hand man.

"Try Harder! Do Better! didn't work because people were already trying their hardest, doing their best! But a certain number of mistakes were built into The System!"

"Of course!" said the left-hand man. "More Inspection! didn't work because people no longer felt responsible for Quality. That was built into The System too!"

The three were onto something now.

"It seems like we ought to change The System," said the right-hand man.

"But how?" asked the left-hand man.

"I'm not sure, offhand," said The Boss. "But one thing I am sure of is that it's our job to figure it out. Management has no other job but to fix The System."

Or so he thought.

And this time he was right.

So they sat down to fix The System.

"Your corollary," said the right-hand man to The Boss, "says that the number of mistakes expands to fill the inspection capacity of The System."

"So if we want to reduce the number of mistakes," said the left-hand man, "we have to reduce the inspection capacity of The System."

The Boss was silent. Thinking.

The right-hand man and the left-hand man looked at each other and smiled. Each had arrived at the same conclusion.

"The way to fix The System," they proclaimed in unison to The Boss, "is to lay off all the new workers we hired as inspectors! Then we have less inspection capacity, and according to your corollary, that means the number of defects will go down! That's the answer!"

They grinned as they got up from the conference table and started for the door to put their idea into action. (Even though both enjoyed being well-liked managers, they enjoyed being tough managers even more. And this was good tough-management stuff. The best!)

"Sit down," said The Boss quietly.

They were disappointed. But they sat.

"You were about to make the biggest mistake of all," said The Boss.

"But your corollary?" they asked.

"My corollary begins with the words 'In a closed system. . . .' But we've already changed The System. We've made a big to-do over Quality. We've doubled the work force. To lay people off would be a breach of faith. It would make morale go down even further.

"If morale goes down, Quality goes down.

"If Quality goes down, market share goes down.

"If market share goes down, profitability goes down.

"And if profitability goes down much further, Punctuation Inc. goes down. For the count."

They were silent for a moment. Then the left-hand man spoke. "You saved us from a serious mistake. That's why you're The Boss," he said.

"And it sure was a lot easier to prevent the mistake from happening in the first place than to have to fix it after the fact," said the right-hand man.

Whapp! The Boss slapped the table with the palm of his hand. "What did you say?!?" he asked the right-hand man excitedly.

The right-hand man wasn't quite sure how to react to The Boss's outburst, but he knew he'd better answer. "I just said," the right-hand man tentatively offered, "it was easier to prevent the mistake than to have to fix it."

"I thought that's what you said," said The Boss.

And then he smiled.

Broadly.

The Boss had been smiling a lot more over the last six months, ever since his right-hand man, with his chance comment, had shown him the light.

"Once we changed our way of thinking from an Inspection to a Prevention mind-set, things began to fall into place," he told himself, with a bemused smile and slow shake of the head.

Quality was up.

Morale was up.

Productivity was up.

Profitability was up.

He was a bit puzzled that market share had only leveled off.

But it *had* stopped falling. (The stand-off, naturally, was with Process Inc.) And it seemed only a matter of time before Process Inc. would join the ranks of all the other vanquished pretenders to Punctuation Inc.'s dominance.

"We've got a handle on our Quality

problems now," he told himself, with a large (and understandable) measure of satisfaction.

And the irony was that the move from Inspection to Prevention had been relatively easy. Once his mind-set had changed.

There was an even bigger irony: What had seemed to be their biggest problem—whatever to do with all those extra people who had been hired as inspectors?—had turned out to be their salvation.

It was so simple, The Boss thought, with another bemused smile and another slow shake of the head.

They had wanted to move from Inspection to Prevention. And they had more inspectors than they knew what to do with. So they had done the obvious thing.

They had made their excess inspectors into preventers.

And it had worked.

Beautifully.

In fact, far more beautifully than they had had reason to hope.

That shouldn't have come as such a big surprise, but it did, thought The Boss, with bemused smile and slow shake number three.

After all, who's in a better position to figure out how to prevent defects than people who are highly skilled at *spotting* defects?

Who better than the people who know the process that *caused* the defects?

The key was in recognizing that our Inspection capacity really formed the solid foundation for our Prevention capacity.

Within days, the new preventers were turning out scads of useful Prevention information. All that was needed then was someone to manage the information that the preventers provided.

That had been easier still. The Boss had put his right-hand man in charge of preventing defects in the design department. And his left-hand man in charge of preventing defects in the manufacturing department.

And each had big success stories to tell.

The left-hand man had devised a way of securing the little hook onto the bottom of a comma so that it wouldn't fall off in mid-sentence. Now customers no longer complained about the hooks falling off, turning their commas into periods. (That had been

nuisance enough when they were writing. But when they were speaking, those sudden stops could cause a bad case of rhetorical whiplash.)

The right-hand man had made a subtle adjustment to the design of brackets, rounding off the sharp edges just enough to eliminate the chance of cut fingers and worker's compensation claims from factory person-

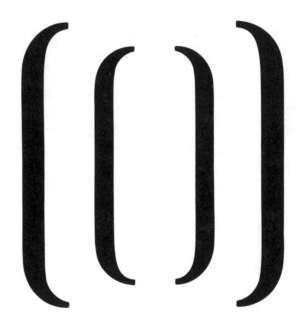

nel, and cut fingers and lawsuits from customers.

"They've done a super job of preventing defects," mused The Boss. "I ought to call them in and tell them so."

And so he did.

"Men," said The Boss to the right-hand man and the left-hand man after they had arrived in his office, "I just want you to know how pleased I am at the progress we've made.

"We saw that we had a Quality problem. All anybody could tell us about Quality was 'I know it when I see it.' Frankly, that wasn't much help. But we persevered.

"First we tried Try Harder! Do Better! But that didn't work because our people were already trying their hardest and doing their best.

"Then we tried More Inspection! But that didn't improve Quality. It just focused on spotting mistakes after they'd already been made.

"Then we saw the light! We changed our mind-sets. We moved from inspecting for defects to preventing defects. And things got better!

"Quality went up!

"Morale went up!

"Productivity went up!

"Profitability went up!

"We're staying even with Process Inc. in market share, but it's only a matter of time before we gain it back! I think we've got our Quality problems licked!"

"It's only a matter of time!" exclaimed the right-hand man.

"We've got the problem licked!" exclaimed the left-hand man.

Or so they thought.

**B**zzzz!" exclaimed The Boss's intercom, interrupting their celebration.

"Yes?" said The Boss.

"There's a customer here to see you," said The Boss's secretary. "Should I tell him to come back later?"

"No, no, no! Send him right in! By all means send him right in!"

The left-hand man and the right-hand man got up to leave.

"Stay here, stay here!" said The Boss, magnanimously. "He's probably here to thank us for providing such a high-quality product. You men ought to share in the praise."

The right-hand man and the left-hand man were pleased.

Then the customer entered. "I have two complaints," he said brusquely.

The right-hand man and the left-hand man were less pleased.

"Complaints? About what?" asked The Boss.

"About the Quality of your products," said the customer.

"I'll bet he doesn't even know what Quality is," whispered the right-hand man to the left-hand man.

"But he'll know it when he sees it," whispered the left-hand man to the right-hand man.

"I want to hear your complaints," said The Boss. "But before that," he added, thinking back to his market research, "would you mind telling me your definition of Quality?"

"I'm not sure, I guess. But I know it when I see it," said the customer.

"It figures," said the sarcastic nods exchanged between the right-hand man and the left-hand man.

"I see," said The Boss, feeling a familiar twinge of exasperation. "Well, what are your specific complaints?"

"Complaint number one has to do with the design of your plus signs," said the customer.

At that the right-hand man stiffened. He

was, after all, responsible for preventing design defects.

"Last month I filed my tax returns," continued the customer. "Somewhere in the mail, the vertical piece of a plus sign must have fallen off. Do you know what you get when you remove the vertical piece from a plus sign—from one of *your* plus signs?" asked the customer.

The Boss thought for a few seconds. "A minus sign?" he offered.

"Exactly. A minus sign. And do you know what else you get?"

"No," said The Boss. And aside from the sinking feeling in the pit of his stomach, that was true. "What else do you get?"

"You get to pay twice as much in taxes! That's what you get! All because of a design defect in your plus signs!"

The Boss looked to the right-hand man. "Do we have an answer?" he asked.

"An easy one," said the right-hand man, very much relieved. "It's not a design problem at all. It's a manufacturing problem. A poor spot weld would be my guess."

The left-hand man gave the right-hand man a dirty look.

"In any event," the right-hand man continued, "you're wrong when you say we have a Quality problem in design."

"Well, whatever," said the customer. "I know Quality when I see it, and that wasn't it."

The Boss was beginning to be concerned. "What's your second complaint?" he asked.

"Complaint number two has to do with how you manufacture your exclamation points," said the customer.

This time it was the left-hand man, who was in charge of preventing defects in manufacturing, who stiffened.

"Go on," said The Boss.

"I was trying to discipline my kids. I wanted to be forceful, so I used some of your exclamation points. I was angry—hot under the collar. So hot that the exclamation points began to melt."

"And?" said The Boss, afraid of what the answer would bring.

"When the exclamation points melted, they turned into question marks!" exclaimed the customer. "So instead of sounding forceful, I sounded weak! Instead of being firm, I was soft! All because of the way you manufacture your product!"

"You sound pretty forceful and strong now," The Boss joked, weakly.

"That's because the exclamation points

I'm using now came from Process Inc.!"
came the clear, pointed reply.

The Boss turned to the left-hand man.

"Do we have an answer?" he asked.

"A simple one," said the left-hand man,
much relieved. "He's wrong. What he per-
ceived as poor Quality in manufacturing is
really a problem in design. Probably a ma-
terials foul-up."

The right-hand man gave the left-hand
man a dirty look.

"Well, whatever," said the customer. "I
know Quality when I see it, and that wasn't
it."

The room fell silent.

The right-hand man was annoyed at
the customer for making ill-founded charges
about the Quality of design.

Ditto the left-hand man about the Quality of manufacturing.

The Boss was disturbed about a bigger issue: Apparently the Quality problem
wasn't licked yet.

Finally The Boss spoke. "Thank you for
taking the time to come in today to tell us
about your concerns," he said to the customer. "You can be sure that we'll take action
to clear up any Quality problems we might
still have."

At this the left-hand man and the right-
hand man gave the customer a dirty look.

"Now," continued The Boss, "is there
anything else we can do for you?"

"Yes," the customer replied, pulling out

a large brown sack. "You can take these back."

And with that, he poured a pile of punctuation marks—Punctuation's punctuation marks—from the sack onto The Boss's desk.

Periods.
Semicolons.
Question marks.
Ellipses.
Dashes.
Parentheses.
Brackets.
Apostrophes.
Asterisks.

You name it, they all poured out of the sack into a dusty black heap.

Finally, one last comma fell out of the sack . . .

rolled down the side of the dusty black heap . . .

skipped across the width of The Boss's desk . . .

and landed on the floor at The Boss's feet.

Plinck.

And with that, the customer left Punctuation Inc.

Literally and figuratively.

The Boss turned to the right-hand man and the left-hand man. "Why don't you two fellows run along?" he said. "I've got some serious thinking to do."

As he said this he smiled a sad smile. The right-hand man and the left-hand man picked up on The Boss's sadness and left without a word, closing the door behind them.

Then The Boss bent down and picked up the comma that had rolled off the dusty black heap and dropped at his feet.

He held it between his thumb and forefinger (by the little hook) and slowly twirled it around and around.

Then he walked over to the portrait of Punctuation Inc.'s founder, and holding the comma up so that his esteemed predecessor could better see it, he said:

"Rufus, old boy, you always said that these could be very powerful little things. I've never doubted that for a minute. But it's only now that I've realized just how right you really were."

He gave the comma one more slow, sad spin. Then he sighed, and sank deep in his chair, deeper in thought.

"Punctuation Inc. is a perfectly fine company," he said aloud. "It's perfectly functional, able to turn out a perfectly utilitarian product.

"But it doesn't sing anymore. It doesn't shine anymore. Somewhere along the way we lost something—or someone took it from us. And I'm not even sure what that something was!"

The Boss gave another sigh. Then he continued.

"We feel the need to be leaders, to be innovators. But somehow our lofty goals get turned into something mundane in the translation.

"We identify a Quality problem and we take action.

"We rally the troops, and somehow that gets translated into lower morale.

"We bolster our Inspection capacity, and somehow that gets translated into more defects.

"We move to a Prevention mind-set, and somehow that gets translated into ex-customers."

The Boss stared right through the dusty black heap of punctuation marks that the ex-customer had dumped on his desk.

He felt like he was at a dead end.

So he did what he always did in such situations. He took pen in hand and wrote out the data that he had to work with.

And he used the format he always used in such situations: "Conversations with Myself" is what The Boss liked to call it.

Here's what he wrote:

1. *Quality is a matter of survival.*

   Above all, I'm certain of this. Sometimes people get caught up with all kinds of fuzzy, abstract "Quality is a warm puppy" notions. That's wrong. Quality is profit and productivity and market share. And that's no warm puppy.

2. *Quality may not be free, but it's a lot less expensive than the alternatives.*

   I never would have believed we could spend so much time and money trying to fix our Quality problems. It would have been a whole lot cheaper had we not had those problems in the first place.

3. *Quality is everyone's job. But it's management's responsibility.*

   Management's job is to lead. Leadership requires two things: movement and followers. And the movement has to come first.

4. *Most Quality problems are built into The System.*

   People want to do high-quality work. And they will if The System will let them. That's where management's movement has to go: toward improving The System.

5. *The first step toward improving The System is to get good data about what needs fixing.*

   Before you can make something good, you have to know what's bad. And the people who are in the best position to have such data are the people with their hands right on the process—the people we used to think of only as inspectors.

6. *The second step toward improving The System is moving from an Inspection mind-set to a Prevention mind-set.*

   In item 2, I said that Quality is a lot less expensive than the alternatives. Well, it's sure a lot less expensive to prevent defects from occurring in the first place than to have some people making them, others finding them, and others fixing them.

At this point The Boss stopped, put

down his pen, and read over what he had written.

"These are all good, valid points," he said. "But if they're so good and valid—if I'm so smart—what is this heap of punctuation marks doing on my desk?"

By now it was quite late. But The Boss couldn't even entertain any thoughts of going home to sleep. At least not until he figured out what the real solution was to Punctuation Inc.'s Quality problems.

"Customers keep telling us we've got Quality problems—that they buy from Process Inc. because of Quality. But they don't even know what Quality is!" The Boss exclaimed in frustration. "Ask them and all they can say is, 'I know it when I see it'!"

The Boss was moving from frustration to anger.

"If they care so much about Quality," his thoughts roared on, "why don't they ask us for our Quality records?

"We've got our specifications, and they're tight specifications! We've got our tolerances, and they're tight tolerances! And we've got records to prove we meet our specs and our tolerances! In fact, I'll bet every one of these meets our specs and tolerances!!"

With that thought The Boss's anger got the best of him. He swept his arm across his desk, scattering the entire dusty black heap across the room.

The entire dusty black heap, that is,

except for a single exclamation point that was left on his desk, directly in front of him.

The Boss cocked his wrist to flick it, too, onto the floor.

But his wrist locked.

"Now I see it!" he exclaimed, putting the exclamation point to use.

"Our customers tell us we have a Quality problem, and we turn to our specs and our tolerances to see if they're 'right.'

"Of course they're right! Customers aren't interested in our specs. They're interested in the answer to one simple question: 'Did the product do what I expected it to do?'

"If the answer is yes, then it's a Quality product. If the answer is no, then it isn't. At that point, our specs and tolerances aren't 'wrong.' They're just irrelevant!"

The Boss was getting very excited. So excited that he wouldn't have been embarrassed had anyone heard him animatedly talking to himself in his office.

"We've had it backwards all along! We've been approaching it as though we were the experts who could rely on some sort of intuitive feel for the ultimate Quality of our products.

"And we'd get impatient with our customers, who couldn't say anything more precise about Quality than 'I know it when I see it.'

"But *they're* the ones entitled to rely on their intuition when it comes to knowing what Quality is.

"They pay *us* to be precise and rigorous about that definition . . . to determine what their requirements are . . . and then to do whatever it takes to meet those requirements.

"They pay *us* to have a firm handle on Quality, and we've been behaving as though it were the other way around!"

Then The Boss began to laugh. Happily, joyfully.

And all the months of work and frustration and bewilderment suddenly were forgotten with this single, crystalline insight.

Thus was Punctuation Inc. reborn.

# Epilogue

"Without further ado, it gives me great pleasure to introduce to you the Quality Man of the Year!"

With that, the master of ceremonies led the applause for The Boss, who was seated at the far end of the dais.

Flashbulbs popped and jewelry shimmered throughout the audience as The Boss made his way to the podium.

His journey took several moments because everyone at the head table wanted to shake The Boss's hand.

And quite a distinguished group it was.

For starters, the President was there.

And the Governor.

Two senators, a congresswoman, and the mayor.

Of course, The Boss's family was there.

And so was his fifth-grade teacher (although no one, least of all The Boss, was quite sure why).

In the audience were hundreds of workers from Punctuation Inc.

And one from Process Inc. (Yes: the woman who resigned from Punctuation Inc. after The Boss's PA pep talk.)

They all stood and cheered and smiled. And it likely would have gone on all night had not The Boss motioned, palms down, for them to be silent and seated.

Then he told them the story they had come to hear.

He told them of how Punctuation Inc. had always been so dominant, so proud of its history and innovation.

He told them about how the company had first dismissed the threat from Process Inc.

"After all, how could they hurt *us*? They never had any ideas of their own!

"Can you imagine our complacency?" said The Boss, chiding himself.

He spoke of how Process Inc. had become impossible to ignore when they had begun to gain market share.

"Taking customers from us that we had assumed were ours by some sort of divine right! Can you imagine our arrogance?" said The Boss, scolding himself.

He spoke of the early attempts at solving the problem, of his frustration at having everyone tell him that Quality was the issue but being able to say nothing more about Quality than "I know it when I see it."

He told them of the attempts at Try Harder! Do Better!

"But how do you ask that of people who are already trying their hardest and doing their best? Foolishly, that's how," said The Boss, mocking himself.

He told them of the attempts at More Inspection!

"Trying to *force* Quality improvements into your process through massive inspection is like trying to squeeze the toothpaste back into the tube. You wind up with a bigger mess than you started with!"

The audience laughed at that. And more than a few of them saw more than a little of themselves in The Boss's litany of false starts and short-term failures.

But then The Boss shifted gears.

"One day we had a real sunburst," he said, his face brightening. "We realized that if we were ever going to make any real progress, we had to change The System. We had to change the way we looked at the world. We had to move from an Inspection mind-set to a Prevention mind-set. We did that. And—lo and behold—we got results."

He told them of how profitability and productivity had improved, and how with them had come an improvement in morale.

Of how market share had only leveled off, but of how they were sure it was only a matter of time before that too turned up.

"It turned out, though, that we were still deluding ourselves. We were still woefully ignorant of the *real* nature of our problems.

"There is one man," he continued solemnly, "who is more responsible for our being here tonight than anyone. Certainly far more responsible than I am. One man who truly showed us the way."

The right-hand man and the left-hand man both sat up a little straighter in their seats, expectantly. They needn't have.

"That man is a customer who walked into my office with two complaints about the Quality of our products. And who then walked away—as an ex-customer.

"He said he had a manufacturing complaint and a design complaint.

"Did we listen to him? I mean *really* listen to him? No. We were too busy clarifying the distinction between design and manufacturing for him."

The Boss gave an ironic shake of the head. "I think that's called winning the battle but losing the war. Who were we to try to 'prove' that we knew more about Quality than our customer did?

"He knew what he bought the product for and whether or not it delivered what he expected. All the specs and tight tolerances and inspection stickers in the world mean nothing next to that judgment!

"And why should he have wanted us to clarify the distinction between design and manufacturing for him? He was paying *us* to know—to care—about those things!"

Again The Boss shook his head. "Apparently, he knew more about what really mattered than we did. Is it any wonder he walked away?"

The Boss paused for a sip of water.

"Later that night—much later that night—it all became clear to me. We had gone from Inspection to Prevention. But we hadn't gone far enough.

"We really didn't have a handle on the Quality issue. And we wouldn't until we viewed Quality as something much, much more than just the 'absence of negatives' and recognized it as something positive— and powerful—in its own right.

"We wouldn't have a handle on the Quality issue until we stopped approaching it with a sort of passive longing and began to attack and manage it in the only way appropriate to an issue so fundamental to our success and survival.

"We weren't there yet by a long shot. For one thing, the problem clearly called for a high level of cooperation and coordination throughout our organization. And—my goodness!—my right-hand man didn't even know what my left-hand man was doing!"

That brought many appreciative chuckles from the audience (not to mention two very sheepish looks).

"It took us a while, but we finally realized that if you've 'fixed' Quality within each department only to have it unravel again as soon as you cross departmental lines, you don't really have a design defect or a manufacturing defect. You've got a *management* defect.

"And that, I'm sure you'll all agree, is the toughest defect of all to fix!"

That brought more appreciative chuckles (and two even more sheepish looks).

"Luckily we figured that out in time," The Boss continued. "In time to get results like these."

And with that the curtain behind The Boss parted dramatically to reveal three charts.

One showed Punctuation Inc.'s productivity up, higher than ever.

One showed Punctuation Inc.'s profitability up, higher than ever.

One showed Punctuation Inc.'s market share up, higher than ever. More dominant than ever.

And from the looks on the faces of Punctuation Inc.'s employees as they stood and cheered, morale too was up, higher than ever.

Once again The Boss quieted the crowd.

"You often hear that 'Quality is everybody's job,' and that's true. But it must start with management. Management's job is to lead people toward a goal. And Quality is the only goal that matters.

"Lead people from an Inspection mindset to a Prevention mind-set. That's an important start. But you've got to go further. You've got to manage Quality as a whole—an integrated whole that is much, much more than the sum of its parts."

The Boss was never better.

"I'd like to leave you with one piece of advice," he continued. "My hope is that I might be able to spare you some of the pain that we went through.

"Above all, listen to what your customers are telling you about Quality. We didn't think they had much to tell us, and we were wrong. Very wrong. Almost dead wrong.

"Listen to the sound of your piece of the market share pie shrinking. That's the sound of your customers telling you about Quality.

"Listen to the sound of your stock price falling because your earnings aren't what you'd hoped they'd be. That's the sound of your customers telling you about Quality.

"Listen to the sound of your work force turning over because people don't like working in a constant atmosphere of crisis and chaos. That's the sound of your customers telling you about Quality.

"Your customers are in a perfect position to tell you about Quality, because that's all they're really buying. They're not buying a product. They're buying your assurances that their expectations for that product will be met.

"And you haven't really got anything

else to sell them *but* those assurances. You haven't really got anything else to sell *but* Quality."

The punctuation marks The Boss was using (from, naturally, Punctuation Inc.) were obviously of high Quality. His message was coming through loud and clear, and the audience was enthralled.

Recognizing this, The Boss knew that it was time to make one final point.

"Your customers may not have all the hard business facts. They may not be aware of your specs and your standards and your inspection reports—all of which are critical to your ability to make a high-quality product.

"But just because they may not be able to speak with a lot of precision, don't assume that what they have to say doesn't have a lot of value.

"They may not be able to give you a precise definition of Quality, but one thing's for certain—they know it when they see it. What's more—" And as he said this he pointed to the charts on the wall behind him, which showed:

Productivity up, way up.

Profitability up, way up.

Market share up, way way up.

And while still pointing to the charts, he summarized for the audience the lesson that had taken him so very long to learn:

"—*you'll* know it when they see it."